DHS PRIVACY OFFICE
2012
DATA MINING REPORT

Table of Contents

I. LEGISLATIVE LANGUAGE

The Federal Agency Data Mining Reporting Act of 2007, 42 U.S.C. § 2000ee-3, includes the following requirement:

(c) Reports on data mining activities by Federal agencies

    (1) Requirement for report - The head of each department or agency of the Federal Government that is engaged in any activity to use or develop data mining shall submit a report to Congress on all such activities of the department or agency under the jurisdiction of that official. The report shall be produced in coordination with the privacy officer of that department or agency, if applicable, and shall be made available to the public, except for an annex described in subparagraph (3).

    (2) Content of report - Each report submitted under subparagraph (A) shall include, for each activity to use or develop data mining, the following information:

        (A) A thorough description of the data mining activity, its goals, and, where appropriate, the target dates for the deployment of the data mining activity.

        (B) A thorough description of the data mining technology that is being used or will be used, including the basis for determining whether a particular pattern or anomaly is indicative of terrorist or criminal activity.

        (C) A thorough description of the data sources that are being or will be used.

        (D) An assessment of the efficacy or likely efficacy of the data mining activity in providing accurate information consistent with and valuable to the stated goals and plans for the use or development of the data mining activity.

        (E) An assessment of the impact or likely impact of the implementation of the data mining activity on the privacy and civil liberties of individuals, including a thorough description of the actions that are being taken or will be taken with regard to the property, privacy, or other rights or privileges of any individual or individuals as a result of the implementation of the data mining activity.

        (F) A list and analysis of the laws and regulations that govern the information being or to be collected, reviewed, gathered, analyzed, or used in conjunction with the data mining activity, to the extent applicable in the context of the data mining activity.

        (G) A thorough discussion of the policies, procedures, and guidelines that are in place or that are to be developed and applied in the use of such data mining activity in order to—

            (i) protect the privacy and due process rights of individuals, such as redress procedures; and

            (ii) ensure that only accurate and complete information is collected, reviewed, gathered, analyzed, or used, and guard against any harmful consequences of potential inaccuracies.[10]

The Act defines "data mining" as:

    a program involving pattern-based queries, searches, or other analyses of 1 or more electronic databases, where—

---

[10] 42 U.S.C. § 2000ee-3(c).

(A) a department or agency of the Federal Government, or a non-Federal entity acting on behalf of the Federal Government, is conducting the queries, searches, or other analyses to discover or locate a predictive pattern or anomaly indicative of terrorist or criminal activity on the part of any individual or individuals;

(B) the queries, searches, or other analyses are not subject-based and do not use personal identifiers of a specific individual, or inputs associated with a specific individual or group of individuals, to retrieve information from the database or databases; and

(C) the purpose of the queries, searches, or other analyses is not solely—

(i) the detection of fraud, waste, or abuse in a Government agency or program;

or

(ii) the security of a Government computer system.[11]

---

[11] 42 U.S.C. § 2000ee-3(b)(1). "[E]lectronic telephone directories, news reporting, information publicly available to any member of the public without payment of a fee, or databases of judicial and administrative opinions or other legal research sources" are not "databases" under the Act. 42 U.S.C. § 2000ee-3(b)(2). Therefore, searches, queries, and analyses conducted solely in these resources are not "data mining" for purposes the Act's reporting requirement. Two aspects of the Act's definition of "data mining" are worth emphasizing. First, the definition is limited to pattern-based electronic searches, queries, or analyses. Activities that use only PII or other terms specific to individuals (e.g., a license plate number) as search terms are excluded from the definition. Second, the definition is limited to searches, queries, or analyses that are conducted for the purpose of identifying predictive patterns or anomalies that are indicative of terrorist or criminal activity by an individual or individuals. Research in electronic databases that produces only a summary of historical trends, therefore, is not "data mining" under the Act.

II. DATA MINING AND THE DHS PRIVACY COMPLIANCE PROCESS

The Department of Homeland Security (DHS) Privacy Office (DHS Privacy Office or Office) is the first statutorily mandated privacy office in the Federal Government. Its mission is to protect all individuals by embedding and enforcing privacy protections and transparency in all DHS activities. The Office works to minimize the impact of DHS programs on an individual's privacy, particularly an individual's personal information, while achieving the Department's mission to protect the homeland. The Chief Privacy Officer reports directly to the Secretary of Homeland Security, and the Office's mission and authority are founded upon the responsibilities set forth in Section 222 of the Homeland Security Act of 2002, as amended (Homeland Security Act).[12]

This is the DHS Privacy Office's seventh comprehensive report to Congress on DHS activities that involve data mining and the fifth report pursuant to the Federal Agency Data Mining Report Act of 2007 (Data Mining Reporting Act).[13] The Homeland Security Act expressly authorizes the Department to use data mining, among other analytical tools, in furtherance of its mission.[14] DHS exercises this authority to engage in data mining in the programs discussed in this report, all of which have been reviewed by the Chief Privacy Officer for potential impacts on privacy. The DHS Chief Privacy Officer's authority for reviewing DHS data mining activities stems from three principal sources: the Privacy Act of 1974, as amended (Privacy Act);[15] the E-Government Act of 2002 (E-Government Act);[16] and Section 222 of the Homeland Security Act, which states that the DHS Chief Privacy Officer is responsible for "assuring that the [Department's] use of technologies sustains, and does not erode, privacy protections relating to the use, collection, and disclosure of personal information."[17] The Office's compliance process discussed below is designed to identify and mitigate risks to privacy that may be posed by any DHS program, project, or information technology system.

The DHS Privacy Office's privacy compliance policies and procedures are based on the Fair Information Practice Principles (FIPPs), which are rooted in the tenets of the Privacy Act and memorialized in the December 2008 *Privacy Policy Guidance Memorandum 2008-01, The Fair*

---

[12] 6 U.S.C. § 142. The authorities and responsibilities of the Chief Privacy Officer were last amended by the 9/11 Commission Act on August 3, 2007. The 9/11 Commission Act added investigative authority, the power to issue subpoenas, and the ability to administer oaths, affirmations, or affidavits necessary to investigate or report on matters relating to responsibilities under Section 222 of the Homeland Security Act. These responsibilities are further described on the DHS Privacy Office website (http://www.dhs.gov/privacy) and in the *DHS Privacy Office 2012 Annual Report to Congress*, available at http://www.dhs.gov/sites/default/files/publications/privacy/Reports/dhs_privacyoffice_2012annualreport_September 2012.pdf.

[13] 42 U.S.C. § 2000ee-3. All of the DHS Privacy Office's Data Mining Reports are available on the DHS Privacy Office website at http://www.dhs.gov/privacy.

[14] The Act states that, "[s]ubject to the direction and control of the Secretary, the responsibilities of the Under Secretary for Information Analysis and Infrastructure Protection, shall be as follows . . . To establish and utilize, in conjunction with the chief information officer of the Department, a secure communications and information technology infrastructure, including data mining and other advanced analytical tools, in order to access, receive, and analyze data and information in furtherance of the responsibilities under this section, and to disseminate information acquired and analyzed by the Department, as appropriate." 6 U.S.C. § 121(d)(13).

[15] 5 U.S.C. § 552a.

[16] Pub. L. No. 107-347.

[17] 6 U.S.C. § 142(a)(1).

Information Practice Principles: Framework for Privacy Policy at the Department of Homeland Security.[18] The FIPPs govern the appropriate use of Personally Identifiable Information (PII) at the Department. DHS uses the FIPPs to enhance privacy protections by assessing the nature and purpose of all PII collected to ensure it fulfills the Department's mission to preserve, protect, and secure the homeland. The Office applies the FIPPs to the full breadth and diversity of Department systems and programs that use PII, including DHS activities that involve data mining.

DHS uses three main documents related to privacy compliance: (1) the Privacy Threshold Analysis (PTA); (2) the Privacy Impact Assessment (PIA);[19] and (3) the System of Record Notice (SORN).[20] While each of these documents has a distinct function in implementing privacy policy at DHS, together these documents further the transparency of Department activities and demonstrate accountability.

- **PTAs:** The PTA is the first document completed by a DHS Component seeking to implement or modify a system, program, technology, project, or rulemaking. The PTA identifies whether the system, program, technology, or project is privacy-sensitive and thus requires additional privacy compliance documentation such as a PIA or SORN.

- **PIAs:** PIAs examine the privacy impact of IT systems, programs, technologies, projects, or rule-makings. PIAs allow the DHS Privacy Office's Compliance Group to review system management activities in key areas such as security and how information is collected, used, and shared. If a PIA is required, the DHS Component will draft the PIA for review by the Component privacy officer or privacy point of contact (PPOC) and component counsel. Part of the PIA analysis includes determining whether an existing SORN appropriately covers the activity or a new SORN is required. Once the PIA is approved at the Component level, the Component privacy officer or PPOC submits it to the DHS Privacy Office Compliance Group for review and approval by the Chief Privacy Officer.

- **SORNs:** SORNs provide notice to the public regarding Privacy Act information collected by a system of records, as well as insight into how information is used, retained, and may be corrected. Part of the Privacy Act analysis requires determining whether certain Privacy Act exemptions should be taken to protect the records from access by an individual for law enforcement or national security reasons. If a SORN is required, the program manager works with the Component privacy officer or PPOC and Component counsel to write a SORN and submits it to the DHS Privacy Office Compliance Group for review and approval by the Chief Privacy Officer.

PTAs, PIAs, and SORNs serve the common purpose of identifying and documenting areas of privacy focus for programs, IT systems, and collections of PII.[21]

---

[18] http://www.dhs.gov/xlibrary/assets/privacy/privacy_policyguide_2008-01.pdf.

[19] The E-Government Act mandates PIAs for all federal agencies when there are new collections of, or new technologies applied to, PII. Pub. L. No. 107-347. As a matter of policy, DHS extends this requirement to all programs, systems, and activities that involve PII or are otherwise privacy-sensitive.

[20] The Privacy Act requires federal agencies to publish SORNs for any group of records under agency control from which information is retrieved by the name of an individual or by an identifying number, symbol, or other identifier assigned to the individual. 5 U.S.C. § 552a(a)(5) and (e)(4).

[21] Once the PTA, PIA, and SORN are completed, the documents are periodically scheduled for a mandatory review by the DHS Privacy Office (timing varies by document type). For systems that require only PTAs and PIAs, the review process begins again three years after the document is complete or when there is an update to the program,

After privacy compliance documentation has been completed and a program, system, or initiative is operational, the DHS Privacy Office also has the authority to monitor and verify ongoing compliance through Privacy Compliance Reviews (PCR) conducted by the Office's Oversight Group. Consistent with the Office's unique role as both an advisory and an oversight body for the Department's privacy-sensitive programs and systems, the PCR is designed as a constructive mechanism for improving compliance with assurances made in existing PIAs, SORNs, or Information Sharing Access Agreements or similar agreements. Department PIAs increasingly include a PCR requirement. For example, U.S. Customs and Border Protection (CBP) and the Privacy Office issued a PIA for CBP's Analytical Framework for Intelligence (AFI), discussed below in Section III.B of this report, which requires that a PCR be completed within 12 months of AFI's deployment.

The DHS Privacy Office identifies DHS programs that engage in data mining through several different processes. The Office reviews all of the Department's Exhibit 300 budget submissions to the Office of Management and Budget (OMB) to learn of programs or systems that use PII and to determine whether they address privacy appropriately.[22] The Office uses the PTA to review all information technology systems that are going through the certification and accreditation (C&A) process required under the Federal Information Security Management Act of 2002 (FISMA)[23] to determine whether they maintain PII. The PIA process also provides the Office insight into technologies used or intended to be used by DHS. In addition, the Office reviews technology investment proposals that the DHS Enterprise Architecture Center of Excellence and Integrated Project Teams process, to ensure that DHS investments in technology include a specific review for compliance with privacy protection requirements. All of these oversight activities provide the Office opportunities to learn about proposed data mining activities and to engage program managers in discussions about potential privacy issues.

The DHS Privacy Office has worked closely with the relevant DHS Components to ensure that privacy compliance documentation required for each program described in this report is current. All of these programs have either issued new or updated PIAs or are in the process of doing so; all are also covered by SORNs.

---

whichever is earlier. The process begins with either the update or submission of a new PTA. The Privacy Act requires that SORNs be reviewed on a biennial basis.

[22] All major DHS IT programs are reviewed by the DHS Privacy Office Compliance Group on an annual basis, prior to submission to OMB for inclusion in the President's annual budget. The Compliance Group plays a substantial role in the review of the OMB budget submissions (known as Exhibit 300s) prior to submission to OMB. *See* Office of Mgmt. & Budget, Executive Office of the President, OMB Circular No. A-11, Section 300, *Planning, Budgeting, Acquisition, and Management of Capital Assets*, available at http://www.whitehouse.gov/sites/default/files/omb/assets/a11_current_year/s300.pdf.

[23] Title 44, U.S.C., Chapter 35, Subchapter III (Information Security).

III. REPORTING

In the 2011 DHS Data Mining Report,[24] the DHS Privacy Office discussed the following Department programs that engage in data mining as defined by the Data Mining Reporting Act:

(1) The Automated Targeting System (ATS), which is administered by CBP and includes modules for inbound (ATS-N) and outbound (ATS-AT) cargo, land border crossings (ATS-L), and passengers (ATS-P); and

(2) The Data Analysis and Research for Trade Transparency System (DARTTS), which is administered by U.S. Immigration and Customs Enforcement (ICE).

This year's report, covering the period December 2011 through December 2012, presents the complete descriptions of ATS-N, ATS-AT, ATS-L, ATS-P, and DARTTS provided in the 2011 DHS Data Mining Report, with updates on modifications, additions, and other developments that have occurred in the current reporting year, including use of ATS by DHS Components other than CBP. The 2011 Report included a brief summary of CBP's Analytical Framework for Intelligence (AFI), which was then in development. This year's report includes a detailed description of AFI as an operational system. In addition, the DHS Privacy Office has identified two new uses of ATS that are discussed below: the vetting of non-immigrant and immigrant visa applications in ATS-P for the U.S. Department of State; and the United States Coast Guard's (USCG) Interagency Operations Center ATS-Enhanced Watchkeeper System.

A. Automated Targeting System (ATS)

1. 2012 Program Update

Several new developments took place with respect to ATS during the reporting period for this report:

a) PIA and SORN Updated

On May 22, 2012, and June 1, 2012, respectively, CBP and the DHS Privacy Office issued an updated SORN and PIA for ATS, to provide greater transparency about existing ATS functions. Specifically, the PIA clarifies core functions of ATS, including those most relevant to this report: (1) comparing information on travelers and cargo arriving in, transiting through, and exiting the United States against law enforcement and intelligence *databases* to identify individuals and cargo requiring additional scrutiny; (2) using targeting rules and rule sets to compare existing information on individuals and cargo with *patterns* (derived from CBP officer experience, analysis of trends or suspicious activity, law enforcement cases, and raw intelligence) that have been identified as requiring additional scrutiny; and (3) ingesting data to minimize the impact of processing searches on operational systems and to act as a back-up for operational systems. The ingestion of data does not change the information accessed by ATS to perform its screening and targeting capabilities, but it does improve the efficiency with which ATS fulfills that mission.[25]

---

[24] http://www.dhs.gov/xlibrary/assets/privacy/dhsprivacy_2011dataminingreport.pdf.

[25] The updated ATS PIA is available at http://www.dhs.gov/xlibrary/assets/privacy/privacy_pia_cbp_ats006b.pdf. The Updated ATS SORN is available at http://www.gpo.gov/fdsys/pkg/FR-2012-05-22/html/2012-12396 htm and in the Federal Register at 77 FR 30297 (May 22, 2012).

b) Non-Immigrant and Immigrant Visa Applications

As the updated PIA explains, ATS-P is now used to vet non-immigrant and immigrant visa applications for the U.S. Department of State (DoS). DoS sends online visa application data to ATS-P for pre-adjudication investigative screening. ATS-P vets the visa application and provides a response to the DoS's Consular Consolidated Database (CCD) indicating whether or not DHS has identified derogatory information about the individual. Applications of individuals for whom derogatory information is identified in ATS-P are either vetted directly in ATS-P if a disposition can be determined without further investigation or additional processing occurs in the ICE Visa Security Program Tracking System (VSPTS-Net) case management system, after which updated information (including relevant case notes) regarding eligibility is provided to both CBP and CCD. The Enhanced Border Security and Visa Entry Reform Act of 2002 (EBSVERA) (Pub. L. 107-173), specifically 8 U.S.C. § 1721, authorizes the use of ATS-P for screening non-immigrant and immigrant visas.

c) ATS-Enhanced Watchkeeper System

During this reporting period the DHS Privacy Office identified one new prospective user of ATS: USCG's Interagency Operations Center (IOC) Watchkeeper System. Watchkeeper is the information sharing and management system software for the IOCs established by the Department to improve multi-agency maritime security operations and enhance cooperation among partner agencies at the nation's 35 most critical ports. Watchkeeper coordinates and organizes port security information to improve tactical decision-making, situational awareness, operations monitoring, rules-based processing, and joint planning in a coordinated interagency environment. Watchkeeper provides a shared operational picture, shared mission tasking, and shared response information sets to all users within an IOC, including partner federal agencies and local port partners.

In 2013, USCG proposes to begin using the ATS-N and ATS-P modules discussed below as tools to conduct pre-arrival screening and vetting of vessel cargo, crew, and passengers. The ATS-enhanced Watchkeeper will provide near real-time data for Captains of the Port (COTP) to better evaluate threats and deploy resources through the active collection of incoming vessel information. With a more detailed picture of the risk profile that a vessel presents, COTPs can make appropriate, informed decisions well ahead of the vessel's arrival in port. USCG legal authorities for the ATS-Enhanced Watchkeeper system include the Security and Accountability for Every Port (SAFE Port) Act of 2006, 46 U.S.C. § 70107A; 5 U.S.C. § 301; 14 U.S.C. § 632; 33 U.S.C. §§ 1223, 1226; 46 U.S.C. §§ 3717, 12501; Section 102 of the Maritime Transportation Security Act of 2002, Pub. L. No. 108-274; Section 102(c) of the Homeland Security Act, 14 U.S.C. § 2; 33 C.F.R. part 160; and 36 C.F.R. chapter XII. The DHS Privacy Office is working closely with the USCG Privacy Office to complete a PIA for Watchkeeper.

d) Secure Flight

TSA's Secure Flight Program (Secure Flight) continued to leverage real-time, threat-based intelligence rules run by ATS-P to identify individuals requiring enhanced screening prior to boarding an aircraft. On the basis of those rules, Secure Flight transmits to the airlines instructions identifying such individuals. More information about Secure Flight is included in the Secure Flight PIA, which was updated most recently on April 13, 2012.[26] An annex to this report containing Sensitive Security Information (SSI) about Secure Flight's use of ATS-P is being provided separately to the Congress. TSA's legal authorities related to passenger screening include 49 U.S.C. §§ 114(d), (e), and (f), and Section 4012(a) of Public Law 108-458 (Intelligence Reform and Terrorism Prevention Act of 2004 (IRTPA)).

e) Overstay Vetting Pilot

The 2011 Data Mining Report discussed the Department-wide Overstay Vetting Pilot, which uses both the United States Visitor and Immigrant Status Indicator Technology (US-VISIT) Program's overstay data (which is maintained in the Arrival and Departure Information System (ADIS)) and ATS-P to identify certain individuals who have remained in the United States beyond their authorized period of admission (overstays) and who may present a heightened security risk.[27] The Department continued the Pilot during this reporting year. The Pilot's goal is to allow ICE to deploy its investigative resources efficiently to locate high-risk overstays and initiate criminal investigations or removal proceedings against those individuals. US-VISIT provides biographical information on identified and possible overstays to CBP, to be run in ATS-P against risk-based rules based on information derived from past investigations and intelligence. CBP returns the results of these analyses to US-VISIT, which, in turn, provides them to ICE for further processing. These activities are covered by PIAs for ATS[28] and the US-VISIT Technical Reconciliation Analysis Classification System.[29] On December 29, 2011, the DHS Privacy Office issued a PIA specific to the Overstay Vetting Pilot to add another layer of analysis to this process that can be updated as the program matures.[30]

Legal authorities for the Overstay Vetting Pilot include: Section 2(a) of the Immigration and Naturalization Service Data Management Improvement Act of 2000, Public Law 106–215; Section 205 of the Visa Waiver Permanent Program Act of 2000, Public Law 106-396; Section 414 of the Uniting and Strengthening America by Providing Appropriate Tools Required to Intercept and Obstruct Terrorism Act (USA PATRIOT Act) of 2001, Public Law 107–56; Section 302 of the EBSVERA; and the Immigration and Nationality Act (INA), 8 U.S.C. §§ 1185, 1225, and 1227 (as delegated by the Secretary of Homeland Security).

---

[26] http://www.dhs.gov/xlibrary/assets/privacy/privacy_pia_tsa_secureflight_update018(e).pdf
[27] 2011 Data Mining Report at p. 6.
[28] See http://www.dhs.gov/xlibrary/assets/privacy/privacy_pia_cbp_ats006b.pdf.
[29] See DHS/NPPD/USVISIT/PIA-004 at http://www.dhs.gov/xlibrary/assets/privacy/privacy_pia_usvisit_tracs.pdf.
[30] The PIA is available at http://www.dhs.gov/xlibrary/assets/privacy/privacy_pia_dhs_odovp.pdf.

f) Air Cargo Advance Screening Pilot

CBP and TSA continued to conduct the Air Cargo Advance Screening (ACAS) joint pilot discussed in last year's Data Mining Report,[31] using existing CBP data collections and ATS-N to identify pre-departure air cargo that may pose a threat to aviation. TSA targeting personnel work side-by-side with CBP targeting personnel to jointly develop rules designed to address threats from air cargo and to review data in ATS. TSA legal authorities for this pilot include 49 U.S.C. § 114(f)(10), which authorizes TSA to ensure the adequacy of security measures for the transportation of cargo, and Section 1602 of the Implementing Recommendations of the 9/11 Commission Act of 2007 (9/11 Commission Act), which amended 49 U.S.C. § 44901 to authorize TSA to screen cargo on passenger and all-cargo aircraft.

2. General ATS Program Description

CBP developed ATS, an intranet-based enforcement and decision support tool that is the cornerstone for all CBP targeting efforts. ATS compares traveler, cargo, and conveyance information against intelligence and other enforcement data by incorporating risk-based targeting rules and assessments. CBP uses ATS to improve the collection, use, analysis, and dissemination of information that is gathered for the primary purpose of targeting, identifying, and preventing potential terrorists and terrorist weapons from entering the United States. CBP also uses ATS to identify other potential violations of U.S. laws that CBP enforces. In this way, ATS allows CBP officers charged with enforcing U.S. law and preventing terrorism and other crimes to focus their efforts on the travelers, conveyances, and cargo shipments that most warrant greater scrutiny. ATS standardizes names, addresses, conveyance names, and similar data so these data elements can be more easily associated with other business data and personal information to form a more complete picture of a traveler, import, or export in context with previous behavior of the parties involved. Traveler, conveyance, and shipment data are processed through ATS and are subject to a real-time, rules-based evaluation.

ATS consists of five modules that focus on exports, imports, passengers and crew (airline passengers and crew on international flights, and passengers and crew on sea carriers), private vehicles crossing at land borders, and a workspace to support the creation and retention of analytical reports. This report discusses all of these modules: ATS-N and ATS-AT (both of which involve the analysis of cargo), ATS-L (which involves analysis of information about vehicles and their passengers crossing the land border), ATS-P (which involves analysis of information about certain travelers), and the ATS Targeting Framework (ATS-TF) (a platform for temporary and permanent storage of data).

The U.S. Customs Service, a legacy organization of CBP, traditionally employed computerized screening tools to target potentially high-risk cargo entering, exiting, and transiting the United States. ATS was originally designed as a rules-based program to identify such cargo; it did not apply to travelers. ATS-N and ATS-AT became operational in 1997. ATS-P became operational in 1999 and is now critically important to CBP's mission. ATS-P allows CBP officers to determine whether a variety of potential risk indicators exist for travelers or their itineraries that may warrant additional scrutiny. ATS-P maintains Passenger Name Record (PNR) data, which is data provided to airlines and travel agents by or on behalf of air passengers

---

[31] 2011 Data Mining Report at p. 6.

seeking to book travel. CBP began receiving PNR data voluntarily from certain air carriers in 1997. Currently, CBP collects this information to the extent it is collected by carriers in connection with a flight into or out of the United States, as part of CBP's border enforcement mission and pursuant to the Aviation and Transportation Security Act of 2001 (ATSA).[32]

ATS ingests various data in real-time from the following DHS and CBP mainframe systems: the Automated Commercial System (ACS), the Automated Manifest System (AMS), the DHS Advance Passenger Information System (APIS), the Automated Export System (AES), the Automated Commercial Environment (ACE), the DHS Electronic System for Travel Authorization (ESTA), the DHS Nonimmigrant Information System (NIIS), DHS Border Crossing Information (BCI), the DHS Student Exchange Visitor Information System (SEVIS) and TECS. TECS includes information from the Federal Bureau of Investigation (FBI) Terrorist Screening Center's (TSC)[33] Terrorist Screening Database (TSDB) and provides access to the Department of Justice's (DOJ) National Crime Information Center (NCIC), which contains information about individuals with outstanding wants and warrants, and to Nlets, a clearinghouse for state wants and warrants as well as information from state Departments of Motor Vehicles (DMV). ATS collects PNR data directly from air carriers. ATS also collects data from certain express consignment services in ATS-N. ATS accesses data from these sources, which collectively include: electronically filed bills of lading (i.e., forms provided by carriers to confirm the receipt and transportation of on-boarded cargo to U.S. ports), entries, and entry summaries for cargo imports; Electronic Export Information (EEI) (formerly referred to as Shippers' Export Declarations) submitted to AES and transportation bookings and bills for cargo exports; manifests for arriving and departing passengers; land border crossing and referral records for vehicles crossing the border; airline reservation data; non-immigrant entry records; records from secondary referrals, incident logs, and suspect and violator indices; seizures; and information from the TSDB and other government databases regarding individuals with outstanding wants and warrants and other high-risk entities. Finally, ATS uses data from Dun & Bradstreet, a commercially available data source, to assist with company identification through name and address matching.

In addition to providing a risk-based assessment system, ATS provides a graphical user interface for many of the underlying legacy systems from which ATS pulls information. This interface improves the user experience by providing the same functionality in a more rigidly controlled access environment than the underlying system. Access to this functionality of ATS uses existing technical security and privacy safeguards associated with the underlying systems.

A large number of rules are included in the ATS modules that encapsulate sophisticated concepts of business activity that help identify potentially suspicious or unusual behavior. The ATS rules are constantly evolving to meet new threats and refine existing rules. When evaluating risk, ATS

---

[32] 49 U.S.C. § 44909. The regulations implementing ATSA are codified at 19 C.F.R. § 122.49d.

[33] The TSC is an entity established by the Attorney General in coordination with the Secretary of State, the Secretary of Homeland Security, the Director of the Central Intelligence Agency, the Secretary of the Treasury, and the Secretary of Defense. The Attorney General, acting through the Director of the FBI, established the TSC in support of Homeland Security Presidential Directive 6 (HSPD-6), dated September 16, 2003, which required the Attorney General to establish an organization to consolidate the Federal Government's approach to terrorism screening and provide for the appropriate and lawful use of terrorist information in screening and law enforcement processes. The TSC maintains the Federal Government's consolidated terrorist watch list, known as the TSDB.

applies the same methodology to all individuals to preclude any possibility of disparate treatment of individuals or groups.

a) ATS-Inbound (ATS-N) and ATS-Outbound (ATS-AT) Modules

i. Program Description

ATS-N assists CBP officers in identifying and selecting for intensive inspection inbound cargo shipments that pose a high risk of containing weapons of mass effect, illegal narcotics, or other contraband. ATS-N is available to CBP officers at all major ports of entry (i.e., air, land, sea, and rail) throughout the United States and also assists CBP personnel in the Container Security Initiative and Secure Freight Initiative decision-making processes.

ATS-AT aids CBP officers in identifying exports that pose a high risk of containing goods requiring specific export licenses, illegal narcotics, smuggled currency, stolen vehicles or other contraband, or exports that may otherwise violate U.S. law. ATS-AT sorts EEI data extracted from AES, compares it to a set of rules, and evaluates it in a comprehensive fashion. This information assists CBP officers in targeting or identifying exports that pose potential aviation safety and security risks (e.g., hazardous materials) or may be otherwise exported in violation of U.S. law.

ATS-N and ATS-AT examine data related to cargo in real time and engage in data mining to provide decision support analysis for the targeting of cargo for suspicious activity. The cargo analysis provided by ATS is intended to add automated anomaly detection to CBP's existing targeting capabilities, to enhance screening of cargo prior to its entry into the United States.

ii. Technology and Methodology

ATS-N and ATS-AT do not collect information directly from individuals. The data used in the development, testing, and operation of ATS-N and ATS-AT screening technology is taken from bills of lading and shipping manifest data provided to CBP through AMS, ACS, ACE, and AES by entities engaged in international trade as part of the existing cargo screening process. The results of queries, searches, and analyses conducted in the ATS-N and ATS-AT system are used to identify anomalous business behavior, data inconsistencies, abnormal business patterns, and potentially suspicious business activity generally. No decisions about individuals are made solely on the basis of these results.

The SAFE Port Act requires ATS to use or investigate the use of advanced algorithms in support of its mission.[34] To that end, as discussed in previous DHS Data Mining Reports, ATS established an Advanced Targeting Initiative, which includes plans for development of data mining, machine learning,[35] and other analytic techniques during the period from FY09 to FY12, for use in ATS-N and ATS-AT. Development is taking place in iterative phases as the databases to be used by this initiative are updated. The various iterations will be deployed to a select user population, which will test the new functionality. The Advanced Targeting Initiative is being undertaken in tandem with ATS' maintenance and operation of the ATS-N and ATS-AT systems. The design and tool-selection processes for data mining, pattern recognition, and

---

[34] 6 U.S.C. § 901.

[35] Machine learning is concerned with the design and development of algorithms and techniques that allow computers to "learn." The major focus of machine learning research is to extract information from data automatically, using computational and statistical methods. This extracted information may then be generalized into rules and patterns.

machine learning techniques in development in the Advanced Targeting Initiative are being evaluated through user acceptance testing by the National Targeting Center (NTC). These system enhancements are principally programming enhancements to automate successful user practices for broader use by ATS users nationally. Upon successful testing, the programming enhancements are included in maintenance and design updates to system operations and deployed on the national level to provide a more uniform enhancement to CBP operations. This practice is being incorporated into future maintenance protocols for ATS.

iii. Data Sources

As noted above, ATS-N and ATS-AT do not collect information directly from individuals. The information maintained in ATS is either collected from private entities providing data in accordance with U.S. legal requirements (e.g., sea, rail, and air manifests) or is created by ATS as part of its risk assessments and associated rules.

ATS-N and ATS-AT use the information in ATS source databases to gather information about importers and exporters, cargo, and conveyances used to facilitate the importation of cargo into and the exportation of cargo out of the United States. This information includes PII concerning individuals associated with imported and exported cargo (e.g., brokers, carriers, shippers, buyers, sellers, exporters, freight forwarders, and crew). ATS-N receives data pertaining to entries and manifests from ACS and ACE, and processes it against a variety of rules to make a rapid, automated assessment of the risk of each import.[36] ATS-AT uses EEI data that exporters file electronically with AES, export manifest data from AES, and export airway bills of lading to assist in formulating risk assessments for cargo bound for destinations outside the United States.

CBP uses commercial off-the-shelf (COTS) software tools to graphically present entity-related information that may represent terrorist or criminal activity, to discover non-obvious relationships across cargo data, to retrieve information from ATS source systems to expose unknown or anomalous activity, and to conduct statistical modeling of cargo-related activities as another method to detect anomalous behavior. CBP also uses custom-designed software to resolve ambiguities in trade entity identification related to inbound and outbound cargo.

iv. Efficacy

Based upon the results of testing and operations in the field, ATS-N and ATS-AT have proved to be effective means of identifying suspicious cargo that requires further investigation by CBP officers. The results of ATS-N and ATS-AT analyses identifying cargo as suspicious have been regularly corroborated by physical searches of the identified cargo.

The goal of the Advanced Targeting Initiative is to enhance CBP officers' ability to identify entities such as organizations, cargo, vehicles, and conveyances with a possible association to terrorism. Leads resulting in a positive, factual determination obtained through further investigation and physical inspections of cargo demonstrate the efficacy of the technologies used in the Initiative. Additionally, successful user acceptance testing has enabled CBP to incorporate

---

[36] ATS-N collects information regarding individuals in connection with the following items including, but not limited to: Sea/Rail Manifests from AMS; Cargo Selectivity Entries and Entry Summaries from the Automated Broker Interface (ABI), a component of ACS; Air Manifests (bills of lading) from AMS; Express Consignment Services (bills of lading); Manifests (bills of lading from Canada Customs and Revenue (CCRA)); CBP Automated Forms Entry Systems (CAFES) CBP Form 7512; QP Manifest Inbound (bills of lading) from AMS; Truck Manifests from ACE; Inbound Data (bills of lading) from AMS; entries subject to Food and Drug Administration Prior Notice requirements from ACS; and Census Import Data from the U.S. Department of Commerce.

certain of these technological enhancements, designed to automate formerly manual practices by CBP officers, into uniform system upgrades to expand the scope of results from past successful practices.

v. Laws and Regulations

There are numerous customs and related authorities authorizing the collection of data regarding the import and export of cargo as well as the entry and exit of conveyances.[37] ATS-AT and ATS-N also support functions mandated by Title VII of Public Law 104-208 (1996 Omnibus Consolidated Appropriations Act for FY 1997), which provides funding for counterterrorism and drug law enforcement. ATS-AT also supports functions arising from the Anti-Terrorism Act of 1987[38] and the 1996 Clinger-Cohen Act.[39] The risk assessments for cargo are also mandated under Section 912 of the SAFE Port Act.[40]

b) ATS-Passenger Module (ATS-P)

i. Program Description

ATS-P is a custom-designed system used at U.S. ports of entry, particularly those receiving international flights and voyages (both commercial and private), and the CBP National Targeting Center to evaluate passengers and crew members prior to their arrival to or departure from the United States. ATS-P facilitates the CBP officer's decision-making process about whether a passenger or crew member should receive additional inspection prior to entry into, or departure from, the country because that person may pose a greater risk for terrorism and related crimes or other crimes. ATS-P is a fully operational application that utilizes CBP's System Engineering Life Cycle methodology[41] and is subject to recurring systems maintenance. ATS-P has no set retirement date.

ii. Technology and Methodology

ATS-P processes traveler information against other information available to ATS, and applies risk-based rules based on CBP officer experience, analysis of trends of suspicious activity, and raw intelligence from DHS and other government agencies, to assist CBP officers in identifying individuals who require additional inspection or in determining whether individuals should be allowed or denied entry into the United States. The risk-based rules are derived from discrete data elements, including criteria that pertain to specific operational or tactical objectives or local enforcement efforts. Unlike in the cargo environment, ATS-P does not use a score to determine an individual's risk level; instead, ATS-P compares information in ATS source databases against watch lists, criminal records, warrants, and patterns of suspicious activity identified through past investigations and intelligence. The results of these comparisons are either assessments of the risk-based rules that a traveler has matched or matches against watch lists, criminal records, or

---

[37] *See, e.g.,* 19 U.S.C. §§ 482, 1431, 1433, 1461, 1496, 1499, 1581-1583; 22 U.S.C § 401; and 46 U.S.C. § 46501.

[38] 22 U.S.C. § 5201 *et seq.*

[39] 40 U.S.C. § 1401 *et seq.*

[40] 6 U.S.C. § 912(b).

[41] CBP's Office of Information & Technology's System Engineering Life Cycle (SELC) is a policy that lays out the documentation requirements for all CBP information technology projects, pilots, and prototypes. All projects and system changes must have disciplined engineering techniques, such as defined requirements, adequate documentation, quality assurance, and senior management approvals, before moving to the next stage of the life cycle. The SELC has seven stages: initiation and authorization, project definition, system design, construction, acceptance and readiness, operations, and retirement.

warrants. The rules are run against continuously updated incoming information about travelers (e.g., information in passenger and crew manifests) from the data sources listed below. While the rules are initially created based on information derived from past investigations and intelligence, data mining queries of data in ATS and its source databases may subsequently be used by analysts to refine or further focus those rules to improve the effectiveness of their application.

The results of queries in ATS-P are designed to signal to CBP officers that further inspection of a person may be warranted, even though an individual may not have been previously associated with a law enforcement action or otherwise noted as a person of concern to law enforcement. The risk assessment analysis is generally performed in advance of a traveler's arrival in or departure from the United States, and becomes another tool available to DHS officers in determining a traveler's admissibility and in identifying illegal activity. In lieu of more extensive manual reviews of traveler information and intensive interviews with every traveler arriving in or departing from the United States, ATS-P allows CBP personnel to focus their efforts on potentially high-risk passengers. CBP does not make decisions about individuals solely based on the results of the data mining of information in ATS-P. Rather, the CBP officer uses the information in ATS-P to assist in determining whether an individual should undergo additional inspection or should be allowed or denied admission into the United States.

iii. Data Sources

ATS-P uses available information from the following databases to assist in the development of the risk-based rules discussed above. ATS-P screening relies upon information in APIS; NIIS, which contains all Form I-94 Notice of Arrival/Departure records and actual ESTA arrivals/departures; ESTA, which contains pre-arrival information for persons traveling from Visa Waiver Program (VWP)[42] countries; the DHS Suspect and Violator Indices (SAVI); and the Department of State visa databases. ATS-P also relies upon PNR information from air carriers, BCI crossing data, seizure data, Report of International Transportation of Currency or Monetary Instrument Form (CMIR) data,[43] and information from the TSDB maintained by the TSC.

iv. Efficacy

ATS-P provides information to its users in near real-time. The flexibility of ATS-P's design and cross-referencing of databases permits CBP personnel to employ information collected through multiple systems within a secure information technology system, in order to detect individuals requiring additional scrutiny. The automated nature of ATS-P greatly increases the efficiency and effectiveness of the officers' otherwise manual and labor-intensive work checking separate databases, thereby facilitating the more efficient movement of travelers while safeguarding the border and the security of the United States. CBP officers use the information generated by ATS-P to aid their decision-making about the risk associated with individuals. As discussed below, ATS includes real-time updates of information from ATS source systems to ensure that CBP officers are acting upon accurate information.

---

[42] The Visa Waiver Program allows eligible foreign nationals from participating countries to travel to the United States for business or pleasure, for stays of 90 days or less, without obtaining a visa. The Program requirements primarily are set forth in the INA, 8 U.S.C. § 1187, and 8 C.F.R. part 217. Section 711 of the 9/11 Commission Act amended Section 217 to strengthen the security of the VWP. ESTA is an outgrowth of that mandate. More information about ESTA is available at http://www.cbp.gov/esta.

[43] The CMIR is the U.S. Department of the Treasury Financial Crimes Enforcement Network (FinCEN) Form 105.

In the past year, ATS-P has identified, through lookouts and/or risk-based rule sets, individuals who were confirmed matches to the TSDB and caused action to be taken to subject them to further inspection or, in some cases, took action to prevent them from boarding. ATS-P matches have also enabled CBP officers and foreign law enforcement partners to disrupt and apprehend persons engaged in human trafficking and drug smuggling operations. For example, CBP officers employed information in ATS-P, in conjunction with advance passenger information, to effect a Visa Waiver Program refusal of admission for three persons suspected of being involved in the Korean sex trade. In another instance, ATS-P was used to compare travel information about two persons initially matched to TECS lookout records upon arrival in Atlanta, Georgia, and to determine that they were traveling companions of a person separately apprehended for drug smuggling in Virginia. Subsequent examination of the two travelers revealed that they, too, were smuggling drugs (2.86 pounds of herion were seized). Finally, a traveler departing California was identified through ATS-P as a match to records linking the traveler to a different traveler, who had been apprehended earlier for smuggling drugs internally. Subsequent review of itinerary and past narcotics smuggling violations led to a more intensive exam of the traveler attempting to depart California, which confirmed internal smuggling of 2.9 pounds of cocaine.

v. Laws and Regulations

CBP is responsible for collecting and reviewing information from travelers entering and departing the United States.[44] As part of this inspection and examination process, each traveler seeking to enter the United States must first establish his or her identity, nationality, and, when appropriate, admissibility to the satisfaction of the CBP officer and then submit to inspection for customs purposes. The information collected is authorized pursuant to the EBSVERA,[45] ATSA, IRTPA, the INA, and the Tariff Act of 1930, as amended.[46] Much of the information collected in advance of arrival or departure can be found on routine travel documents that passengers and crew members may be required to present to a CBP officer upon arrival in or departure from the United States.

c) ATS-Land Module (ATS-L)

i. Program Description

ATS-L provides CBP Officers and Border Patrol Agents at the land border with access to real-time screening and targeting databases to assess the risk posed by vehicles and their occupants, as well as pedestrians, as they cross the border. The module employs data obtained from CBP license plate readers and traveler documents to compare information against state DMV databases and ATS screening datasets to assess risk and to determine if a vehicle or its passengers may warrant further scrutiny. This analysis permits the officer or agent to prepare for the arrival of the vehicle at initial inspection and to assist in determining which vehicles might warrant referral for further evaluation. ATS-L's real-time assessment capability improves security at the land border while expediting legitimate travelers through the border crossing process.

---

[44] *See, e.g.*, 19 U.S.C. §§ 482, 1431, 1433, 1461, 1496, 1499, 1581-1583; 8 U.S.C. §§ 1221, 1357; 46 U.S.C. § 46501; and 49 U.S.C. § 44909.
[45] Pub. L. No. 107-173.
[46] 19 U.S.C. §§ 66, 1433, 1454, 1485, and 1624.

ii. Technology and Methodology

ATS-L processes vehicle, vehicle occupant, and pedestrian information against other data available to ATS, and applies rules developed by subject matter experts (officers and agents drawing upon years of experience reviewing historical trends and current threat assessments), system learning rules (rules resulting from the system's weighting positive and negative results from subject matter expert rules), or affiliate rules (derived from data establishing an association with a known violator). The subject matter expert rules are derived from discrete data elements, including criteria that pertain to specific operational or tactical objectives or local enforcement efforts. ATS-L also compares license plate and DMV data to information in ATS source databases including watch lists, criminal records, warrants, and a statistical analysis of past crossing activity. The results of these comparisons are either assessments recommending further official interest in a vehicle and its occupants or supporting information for the clearance and admission of the vehicle and its occupants.

The results of positive queries in ATS-L are designed to signal to DHS officers that further inspection of a vehicle or its occupants may be warranted, even though an individual may not have been previously associated with a law enforcement action or otherwise noted as a person of concern to law enforcement. The risk assessment analysis at the border is intended to permit a recommendation prior to the vehicle's arrival at the point of initial inspection, and becomes one more tool available to DHS officers in determining admissibility and in identifying illegal activity. In lieu of more extensive manual reviews of a person's information and intensive interviews with each occupant of a vehicle or pedestrian arriving in the United States, ATS-L allows DHS personnel to focus their efforts on potentially high-risk vehicles and occupants. DHS does not make decisions about individuals based solely on the information in ATS-L. Rather, the DHS officer uses the information in ATS-L to assist in determining whether an individual should undergo additional inspection or be allowed admission into the United States.

iii. Data Sources

ATS-L uses available information from the following databases to assist in the development of the risk-based rules discussed above. ATS-L screening relies upon information in NIIS, ESTA, SAVI, and the Department of State visa databases. ATS-L also relies upon TECS crossing data, seizure data, feeds from Nlets (formerly the National Law Enforcement Telecommunications System), NCIC, SEVIS, and information from the TSDB maintained by the TSC.

iv. Efficacy

ATS-L provides information to its users in real time, permitting an officer to assess his or her response to the crossing vehicle or pedestrian prior to initiating the border crossing process. The automated nature of ATS-L is a significant benefit to officer safety by alerting officers of potential threats prior to the vehicle's arrival at the point of inspection. It also greatly increases the efficiency and effectiveness of the officer's otherwise manual and labor-intensive work checking individual databases, thereby facilitating the more efficient movement of vehicles, their occupants, and pedestrians, while safeguarding the border and the security of the United States. CBP officers use the information generated by ATS-L to aid their decision-making about risk associated with vehicles, their occupants, and pedestrians. As discussed above, ATS includes real-time updates of information from ATS source systems to ensure that CBP officers are acting upon accurate information.

v. Laws and Regulations

CBP is responsible for collecting and reviewing information about vehicles and their occupants prior to entering the United States.[47] As part of this inspection and examination process, the occupants of each vehicle seeking to enter the United States must first establish their identity, nationality, and, when appropriate, admissibility to the satisfaction of the CBP officer and must submit to inspection for customs purposes. Information collection in ATS-L is pursuant to the authorities for information collection in ATS-P (i.e., EBSVERA;[48] ATSA; IRTPA; the INA, and the Tariff Act of 1930, as amended). Much of the information collected in advance of or at the time of arrival can be found on routine travel documents possessed by the occupants (which they may be required to present to a CBP officer upon arrival in the United States), the vehicle's license plate, and official records pertaining to the registry of the vehicle.

3. ATS Privacy Impacts and Privacy Protections

The Privacy Office has worked closely with CBP to ensure that ATS satisfies the privacy compliance requirements for operation. As noted above, CBP completed an updated PIA and SORN for ATS in June 2012. CBP, the DHS Privacy Office, the DHS Office for Civil Rights and Civil Liberties, and the DHS Office of the General Counsel conduct joint quarterly reviews of the risk-based targeting rules used in ATS to ensure that the rules are appropriate, relevant, and effective.

Authorized CBP officers and personnel from ICE, TSA, and U.S. Citizenship and Immigration Services (USCIS) who are located at seaports, airports, land border ports, and operational centers around the world use ATS to support targeting-, inspection-, and enforcement-related requirements.[49] ATS supports, but does not replace, the decision-making responsibility of CBP officers and analysts. Decisions made or actions taken regarding individuals are not based solely upon the results of automated searches of data in the ATS system. Information obtained in such searches assists CBP officers and analysts in either refining their analysis or formulating queries to obtain additional information upon which to base decisions or actions regarding individuals crossing U.S. borders.

ATS relies upon its source systems to ensure the accuracy and completeness of the data they provide to ATS. When a CBP officer identifies any discrepancy regarding the data, the officer will take action to correct that information, when appropriate. ATS monitors source systems for changes to the source system databases. Continuous source system updates occur in real time, or near-real time, from TECS, which includes data accessed from NCIC and Nlets, as well as from ACE, AMS, ACS, AES, ESTA, NIIS, BCI, SEVIS, and APIS. When corrections are made to data in source systems, ATS updates this information in near-real time and uses only the latest data. In this way, ATS integrates all updated data (including accuracy updates) in as close to real time as possible.[50]

---

[47] *See, e.g.*, 19 U.S.C. §§ 482, 1431, 1433, 1461, 1496, 1499, 1581-1583; 8 U.S.C. §§ 1221, 1357; 22 U.S.C. § 401; 46 U.S.C. § 46501; and 49 U.S.C. § 44909.

[48] Pub. L. No. 107-173.

[49] TSA, ICE, USCIS, and personnel from the DHS Office of Intelligence and Analysis (I&A) have access only to a limited version of ATS. I&A personnel use ATS in support of their authorized intelligence activities in accordance with applicable law, Executive Orders, and policy.

[50] To the extent information that is obtained from another government source is determined to be inaccurate, this problem would be communicated to the appropriate government source for remedial action.

In the event that PII (such as certain data within a PNR) used by or maintained in ATS-P is believed by the data subject to be inaccurate, a redress process has been developed. The individual is provided information about this process during examination at secondary inspection. CBP officers have a brochure available to each individual entering and departing the United States that provides CBP's Pledge to Travelers. This pledge gives each traveler an opportunity to speak with a passenger service representative to answer any questions about CBP procedures, requirements, policies, or complaints.[51] CBP has created the CBP INFO Center in its Office of Public Affairs to serve as a clearinghouse for all redress requests, which come to CBP directly and concern inaccurate information collected or maintained by its electronic systems, including ATS. This process is available even though ATS does not form the sole basis for identifying enforcement targets. To facilitate the redress process, DHS has created a comprehensive, Department-wide program, the Traveler Redress Inquiry Program (DHS TRIP), to receive all traveler-related comments, complaints, and redress requests affecting its component agencies. Through DHS TRIP, travelers can seek redress regarding difficulties they experience during inspection by CBP.[52]

Under the ATS PIA and SORN, and as a matter of DHS policy, CBP permits any subject of PNR or his or her representative to make administrative requests for access and amendment of the PNR. Procedures for individuals to access ATS information are outlined in the ATS SORN and PIA. These procedures mirror the procedures providing for access in the source systems for ingested data, so that individuals may gain access to their own data from either ATS or the source systems that provide input to ATS in accordance with the procedures set out in the SORN for each source system. The Freedom of Information Act (FOIA) provides an additional means of access to PII held in source systems.[53] Privacy Act and FOIA requests for access to information for which ATS is the source system are directed to CBP.[54]

ATS underwent the C&A process in accordance with DHS and CBP policy and obtained its initial C&A on June 16, 2006. ATS also completed a Security Risk Assessment on March 28, 2006, in compliance with FISMA, OMB policy, and National Institute of Standards and Technology guidance. The ATS C&A and Security Risk Assessment were subsequently updated and are valid until January 21, 2014.

Access to ATS is audited periodically to ensure that only appropriate individuals have access to the system. CBP's Office of Internal Affairs also conducts periodic reviews of ATS to ensure that the system is being accessed and used only in accordance with documented DHS and CBP policies. Access to the data used in ATS is restricted to persons with a clearance approved by CBP, approved access to the separate local area network, and an approved password. All CBP process owners and all system users are required to complete annual training in privacy awareness and must pass an examination. If an individual does not take training, that individual loses access to all computer systems, including ATS. As a condition precedent to obtaining

---

[51] In addition, travelers can visit CBP's INFO Center website at http://www.cbp.gov/xp/cgov/travel/customerservice/ to request answers to questions and submit complaints electronically. This website also provides travelers with the address of the CBP INFO Center and the telephone number of the Joint Intake Center.

[52] DHS TRIP can be accessed at: http://www.tsa.gov/traveler-information/dhs-traveler-redress-inquiry-program-dhs-trip.

[53] 5 U.S.C. § 552.

[54] Requests may be submitted by mail to FOIA Division, 799 9th Street NW, Mint Annex, Washington, DC 20229-1177, by email to CBPFOIA@dhs.gov, or by phone to the CBP FOIA office is (202) 325-0150.

access to ATS, CBP employees are required to meet all privacy and security training requirements necessary to obtain access to TECS.

As discussed above, ATS both collects information directly and derives other information from various systems. To the extent information is collected from other systems, data is retained in accordance with the record retention requirements of those systems.

The retention period for data maintained in ATS will not exceed fifteen years, after which time it will be disposed of in accordance with ATS' National Archives and Records Administration (NARA)-approved record retention schedule, except as noted below.[55] The retention period for PNR, which is contained only in ATS-P, will be subject to the following further access restrictions and masking requirements: ATS-P users with PNR access will have access to PNR in an active database for up to five years, with the PNR depersonalized and masked after the first six months of this period. After the initial five-year retention period in the active database, the PNR will be transferred to a dormant database for a period of up to ten years. Within the dormant database, PNR will be accessible for criminal matters for up to five years but will remain available for counterterrorism purposes for the full duration of its 15-year retention. PNR in dormant status will be subject to additional controls including the requirement of obtaining access approval from a senior DHS official designated by the Secretary of Homeland Security. Furthermore, PNR in the dormant database may only be re-personalized in connection with a law enforcement operation and only in response to an identifiable case, threat, or risk.[56]

Notwithstanding the foregoing, information maintained only in ATS that is linked to law enforcement lookout records, and CBP matches to enforcement activities, investigations, or cases (i.e., specific and credible threats; flights, individuals, and routes of concern; or other defined sets of circumstances) will remain accessible for the life of the law enforcement matter to support that activity and other enforcement activities that may become related.

B. Analytical Framework for Intelligence (AFI)

1. 2012 Program Update
The 2011 Data Mining Report briefly noted that CBP was then developing the Analytical Framework for Intelligence (AFI) to augment CBP analysts' ability to review the data in ATS source systems and improve the risk-based rules used by ATS to identify individuals who may pose a heightened security risk.[57] CBP and the DHS Privacy Office published a PIA and SORN for AFI on June 1, 2012, and June 7, 2012, respectively, and AFI became operational in August 2012.[58]

2. Program Description
AFI enhances CBP's ability to identify, apprehend, and prosecute individuals who pose a potential law enforcement or security risk, and aids in the enforcement of customs and

---

[55] NARA approved the record retention schedule for ATS on April 12, 2008.

[56] These masking requirements have been implemented pursuant to the U.S.-E.U. PNR Agreement entered into force on June 1, 2012. The Agreement is available on the Privacy Office website at http://www.dhs.gov/privacy-foia-reports#5.

[57] 2011 Data Mining Report at p. 17.

[58] The PIA for AFI is available at http://www.dhs.gov/xlibrary/assets/privacy/privacy_pia_cbp_afi_june_2012.pdf. The AFI SORN is available at http://www.gpo.gov/fdsys/pkg/FR-2012-06-07/html/2012-13813.htm and in the Federal Register at 77 FR 33753 (June 7, 2012).

immigration laws, and other laws enforced by CBP at the border. AFI is used for the purposes of: (1) identifying individuals, associations, or relationships that may pose a potential law enforcement or security risk, targeting cargo that may present a threat, and assisting intelligence product users in the field in preventing the illegal entry of people and goods, or identifying other violations of law; (2) conducting additional research on persons or cargo to understand whether there are patterns or trends that could assist in the identification of potential law enforcement or security risks; and (3) sharing finished intelligence products[59] developed in connection with the above purposes with DHS employees who have a need to know in the performance of their official duties and who have appropriate clearances or permissions, or externally pursuant to routine uses in the AFI SORN.

AFI augments CBP's ability to gather and develop information about persons, events, and cargo of interest by creating an index of the relevant data in the existing operational systems and providing AFI analysts with different tools that assist in identifying non-obvious relationships. AFI allows analysts to generate finished intelligence products to better inform finished intelligence product users about why an individual or cargo may be of greater security interest based on the targeting and derogatory information identified in or through CBP's existing data systems. CBP currently utilizes transaction-based systems such as TECS and ATS for targeting and inspections. AFI enhances the information from those systems by utilizing different analytical capabilities and tools that provide link analysis among data elements as well as the ability to detect trends, patterns, and emerging threats.

AFI improves the efficiency and effectiveness of CBP's research and analysis process by providing a platform for the research, collaboration, approval, and publication of finished intelligence products. AFI analysts use AFI to conduct research on individuals, cargo, or conveyances to understand whether there are patterns that could assist in the identification of potential law enforcement or security risks.

AFI provides a set of analytic tools that include advanced search capabilities into existing DHS sources, and federated queries to other federal agency sources and commercial data aggregators, to allow analysts to search several databases simultaneously. AFI tools scan the query results, associate and extract similar themes, and present the results to the AFI analyst in a manner that allows for easy visualization and analysis.

In order to enable faster return of search results, AFI creates an index of the relevant data in existing operational DHS source systems by ingesting this data from source data systems, as described below. AFI also permits AFI analysts to upload and store information that may be relevant from other sources, such as the Internet or traditional news media. Requests for Information (RFI), responses to RFIs, finished intelligence products, and unfinished "projects"[60] are also part of the index. The indexing engines refresh data from the originating system periodically depending on the source data system. AFI adheres to the records retention policies of the source data systems along with their user access controls.

AFI analysts are able to perform searches with more efficacy in AFI because the data has been indexed, which allows for a search across all identifiable information in a record. Within AFI,

---

[59] "Finished Intelligence Products" are tactical, operational, and strategic law enforcement intelligence products that have been reviewed and approved for sharing with finished intelligence product users and authorities outside DHS.
[60] AFI analysts create "projects" within the AFI workspace to capture research and analysis that is in progress and may or may not lead to a finished intelligence product or RFI response.

this is a quick search that shows where a particular individual or characteristic arises. With other systems, a similar search for a particular individual requires several queries across multiple systems to retrieve a corresponding response.

AFI also enables analysts to perform federated queries against external data sources, including the Department of State, DOJ/FBI, and commercial data aggregators. AFI tracks where AFI analysts search and routinely audits these records. AFI analysts use data that is available from commercial data aggregators to complement or clarify the data they have access to within DHS. AFI provides a suite of tools that assist analysts in detecting trends, patterns, and emerging threats, and in identifying non-obvious relationships, using the information maintained in the index and made accessible through the federated query.

AFI also serves as a workspace that allows AFI analysts to create finished intelligence products, to maintain and track projects throughout their lifecycle from inception to finished intelligence product or from RFI to response, and to share finished intelligence products either within DHS or externally through regular law enforcement and intelligence channels to authorized users with a need to know, pursuant to routine uses in the AFI SORN.[61]

3. Technology and Methodology

AFI creates and retains an index of searchable data elements in existing operational DHS source systems by ingesting this data through and from its source systems. The index indicates which source system records match the search term used. AFI maintains the index of the key data elements that are personally identifiable in source data systems. If, however, a particular source data system is not available because of technical issues, the AFI analyst will not be able to retrieve the entirety of the responsive record. The indexing engines refresh data from the source system periodically. Any changes to source system records, or the addition or deletion of source system records, will be reflected in corresponding amendments to the AFI index as the index is routinely updated.

AFI includes a suite of tools designed to give AFI analysts visualization, modeling, collaboration, analysis, summarization, and reporting capabilities. These include text analysis, link analysis (social network analysis), statistical analysis, and geospatial analysis.

Specific types of analysis include:

- *Statistical analysis*: Statistical analysis provides modeling and statistical tools that can help analysts discover patterns or generalizations in the data. This analysis can produce models that can be used to identify similar patterns in other data or common characteristics among seemingly disparate data.

- *Geospatial analysis*: Geospatial analysis utilizes visualization tools to display a set of events or activities on a map showing streets, buildings, geopolitical borders, or terrain. This analysis can help produce intelligence about the location or type of location that is favorable for a particular activity.

- *Link analysis*: Link analysis provides visualization tools that can help analysts discover patterns of associations among various entities. This analysis can produce a social network representation of the data.

---

[61] A detailed description of the processes leading to finished intelligence products and RFI responses is included in the PIA for AFI.

- *Temporal analysis*: Temporal analysis offers visualization tools that can display events or activities in a timeline to help an analyst identify patterns or associations in the data. This analysis can produce a time sequence of events that can be used to predict future activities or discover other similar types of activities.

The results of these analyses are used to generate finished intelligence products, responses to RFIs, and projects. The finished intelligence products are published in AFI for finished intelligence product users to search. Several forms of the analyses involve aspects of data mining; both the statistical and link analyses employ characteristics of behavior, associations, or circumstances to identify patterns of activity or networks. In all situations, research developed or reports created by AFI analysts are subject to supervisory review to confirm a rational relationship between the subject of a query and the responsive information. This review also extends to the scope and context of the responsive information to ensure that a compiled report remains germane to its initial purpose. Further consideration is given to the intended audience of a product or report. AFI does not permit dissemination within its user community of products or reports that lack supervisory approval. No decisions about individuals are made exclusively on the basis of the results of research obtained from AFI.

4. Data Sources

The AFI system does not collect information directly from the public. Rather, AFI performs searches for and accesses information collected and maintained in other systems, including information from both government-owned sources and commercial data aggregators. Additionally, AFI analysts may upload information that they believe is relevant to a project, including information publicly available on the Internet. AFI uses, disseminates, or maintains six categories of data containing PII:

- *DHS-Owned Data*: AFI automatically collects and stores selected data from DHS systems. This data is indexed and then as information is retrieved via a search, data from multiple sources may be joined to create a more complete representation of an event or concept. For example, a complex event such as a seizure that is represented by multiple records may be composed into a single object for display. AFI receives records from:
  - ATS (including: APIS; ESTA; TECS Incident Report Logs and Search, Arrest, Seizure Reports, Primary Name Query, Primary Vehicle Query, Secondary Referrals, TECS Intel Documents; and visa data);
  - Enterprise Management Information System-Enterprise Data Warehouse (EMIS-EDW) (including: Arrival and Departure Form I-94; CMIR data; apprehension, inadmissibility, and seizure information from the ICE Immigration and Enforcement Operational Records System (ENFORCE); National Security Entry-Exit Program information from ENFORCE; SEVIS information; and seizure information from the Seized Asset and Case Tracking System); and
  - case information from the Targeting Framework.

- *Other Government Agency Data*: AFI obtains imagery data from the National Geospatial-Intelligence Agency and obtains other government agency data to the extent available through ATS, such as identity and biographical information, wants and warrants, DMV data, and data from the TSDB.[62]

- *Commercial Data*: AFI collects identity and imagery data from several commercial data aggregators so that DHS AFI analysts can cross-reference that information with the information contained in DHS-owned systems. Commercial data aggregators include sources available by subscription only that connect directly to AFI, and do not include information publicly available on the Internet.

- *AFI Analyst-Provided Information*: This includes any information uploaded by an authorized user either as original content or from an *ad hoc* data source such as the Internet or traditional news media. AFI analyst-provided information may include textual data (such as official reports users have seen as part of their duties or segments of a news article), video and audio clips, pictures, or any other information the user believes is relevant. User-submitted RFIs and projects are also stored within AFI, as well as the responses to those requests.

- *AFI Analyst-Created Information*: AFI maintains user-created projects as well as finished intelligence products. Finished intelligence products are made available through AFI to finished intelligence users.

- *Index Information*: As noted above, AFI ingests subsets of data from CBP and DHS systems to create an index of searchable data elements. The index indicates which source system records match the search term used.

The data elements that may be maintained in these six categories include: full name, date of birth, gender, travel information, passport information, country of birth, physical characteristics, familial and other contact information, importation/exportation information, and enforcement records. DHS data sources utilized in AFI are all unclassified.

5. Efficacy

AFI became operational in August 2012. CBP has since sought to deploy AFI to field and headquarters locations to assign officers, agents, and employees user roles and to provide training commensurate with those roles. Initial testing and operational use of AFI along the Southwest border have shown that AFI provides valuable assistance to ongoing operations. Further information on the efficacy of AFI in supporting Department operations will be included in future Data Mining Reports.

6. Laws and Regulations

Numerous authorities mandate that DHS and CBP provide border security and safeguard the homeland, including: Title II of the Homeland Security Act (Pub. L. 107-296), as amended by IRTPA; the Tariff Act of 1930, as amended; the INA (8 U.S.C. § 1101, et seq.); the 9/11 Commission Act (Pub. L. 110-53); the Antiterrorism and Effective Death Penalty Act of 1996 (Pub. L. 104-132); the SAFE Port Act; ATSA; and 6 U.S.C. § 202.

7. Privacy Impact and Privacy Protections

CBP does not use the information in AFI to make unevaluated automated decisions about individuals. Given the breadth of the data available to AFI users, CBP has built extensive

---

[62] A more complete discussion of other government agency data that may be accessed through ATS can be found in the ATS PIA.

privacy protections into the structure and governance of AFI.[63] AFI does not collect information directly from individuals; AFI source systems are responsible, where appropriate, for providing individuals an opportunity to decline to provide information or to consent to or opt out of use information. AFI provides the public notice about its use of information through its PIA and SORN.

AFI is being designed and developed in an iterative, incremental fashion. CBP has created a governance board to ensure that AFI is built and used in a manner consistent with the Department's authorities and that information in AFI is used consistent with the purpose for which it was originally collected. The governance board includes representatives from CBP's Office of Intelligence and Investigative Liaison, Office of Field Operations, Office of Chief Counsel, Office of Information Technology, and the CBP Privacy Office, who review requested changes to the system on a quarterly basis and determine whether additional input is required. The governance board will direct the development of new aspects of AFI, and review and approve new or changed uses of AFI, new or updated user types, and new or expanded data to be made available in or through AFI. As an added layer of oversight, the DHS Privacy Office will conduct a PCR for AFI beginning in August 2013, as stated in the AFI PIA, and may continue to do so thereafter as circumstances dictate.

Although AFI indexes information from many different source data systems, each source system maintains control of the data that it originally collected, even though the data is co-located in both the source system and in AFI. Accordingly, only DHS AFI analysts authorized to access the data in a particular source system have access to that same data through AFI.[64] This is accomplished by passing individual user credentials from the originating system or through a previously approved certification process in another system. Finished intelligence product users and DHS AFI analysts have access to finished intelligence products, but only DHS AFI analysts have access to the source data, projects, and analytical tools maintained in AFI. In order to access AFI, all AFI users are required to complete biannual training in privacy awareness and the privacy training required of all CBP employees with access to CBP's law enforcement systems. This training is regularly updated. Users who do not complete this training lose access to all computer systems, including AFI.

As AFI does not collect information directly from the public or any other primary source, it depends on the system(s) performing the original collection to ensure data accuracy. DHS AFI analysts will use a variety of data sources available through the source systems to verify and correlate the available information to the greatest extent possible. The accuracy of DHS-owned data, other federal agency data, and data provided by commercial data aggregators is dependent on the original source. DHS AFI analysts are required by policy to make changes to the data records in the underlying DHS system of record if they identify inaccurate data and alert the source agency of the inaccuracy. AFI will then reflect the corrected information. Additionally, as the source systems for other federal agency data or commercial data aggregators correct information, queries of those systems will reflect the corrected information.

---

[63] The PIA for AFI includes a more complete description of these protections.

[64] Only authorized CBP personnel and analysts who require access to the functionality and data in AFI as a part of the performance of their official duties and who have appropriate clearances or permissions will have access to AFI.

In order to further mitigate the risk of AFI's retaining incorrect, inaccurate, or untimely information, AFI routinely updates its index to ensure that only the most current data are available to its users. Any changes to source system records, or the addition or deletion of a source system record, is reflected in the corresponding amendments to the AFI index when the index is updated. Further, when a user accesses individual records, the records are retrieved directly from the source system to ensure data quality. AFI also requires that users recertify annually any user-provided information marked as containing PII to ensure its continued relevance and accuracy. If the information is not recertified, it is automatically purged from the system.

AFI has built-in system controls that identify what particular users are able to view, query, or write, as well as audit functions that are routinely reviewed. AFI uses security and auditing tools to ensure that information is used in accordance with CBP policies and procedures. The security and auditing tools include: *Role-Based Access Control*, which determines a user's authorization to use different functions, capabilities, and classifications of data within AFI, and *Discretionary Access Control*, which determines a user's authorization to access individual groupings of user-provided data. Data are labeled and restricted based on data handling designations for Sensitive but Unclassified data (e.g., For Official Use Only, SSI, LES) and based on need to know.

AFI has been developed to Intelligence Community Protection Level 2+ (PL2+) standards to prevent unauthorized access to data, ensuring that isolation between users and data is maintained based on need-to-know. Application logging and auditing tools monitor data access and usage, as required by the information assurance policies against which AFI was designed, developed, and tested (including Director of Central Intelligence (DCID) 6/3 and DHS Management Directive 4300 A/B). AFI received its C& A, and was granted a three-year authority to operate (ATO) from DHS IT Security, in November 2010. The government systems accessed or used by AFI have undergone C&A and are covered by their respective ATOs.

As AFI contains sensitive information related to intelligence, counterterrorism, homeland security, and law enforcement programs, activities, and investigations, DHS has exempted AFI from the access and amendment provisions of the Privacy Act of 1974, pursuant to 5 U.S.C. §§ 552a(j)(2) and (k)(2). For index data and source data, as described in the SORN for AFI, to the extent that a record is exempted in a source system, the exemption will continue to apply. Where there is no exemption for giving access to a record in a source system, CBP will provide access to that information maintained in AFI.[65]

AFI adheres to the records retention policies of its source data systems. AFI is in the process of completing NARA requirements for data retention to obtain a records schedule. AFI is proposing that projects be retained for up to 30 years, RFIs and responses to RFIs for 10 years, and finished intelligence products for 20 years. These retention periods would be commensurate with those in

---

[65] Notwithstanding the applicable exemptions, CBP reviews all requests for access to records in AFI on a case-by-case basis. Where such a request is made, and access would not appear to interfere with or adversely affect the national or homeland security of the United States or activities related to any investigatory material contained within this system, the applicable exemption may be waived at the discretion of CBP, and in accordance with procedures published in the applicable SORN. Requests may be submitted to U.S. Customs and Border Protection, Freedom of Information Act (FOIA) Division, Mint Annex Building, 1300 Pennsylvania Avenue, NW, Washington, DC 20229. Additional information on submitting FOIA and Privacy Act requests is included in the PIA for AFI at pp.22-23.

place for similar records in DHS.

C. Data Analysis and Research for Trade Transparency System (DARTTS)

1. 2012 Program Update

On April 2, 2012, ICE published a PIA Update for DARTTS to address several changes to the system, including: (1) the addition of two new data sets; (2) the expansion of DARTTS to permit select CBP Officers and import specialists to access the system; and (3) the creation of a separate instance of DARTTS for use by foreign government partners.[66]

The 2011 DHS Data Mining Report noted that ICE added two data sources – the Specially Designated Nationals List (SDN List) and TECS subject records – to DARTTS during the 2011 reporting period. The 2011 Report also addressed ICE's plans to expand the use of DARTTS to include select CBP Officers and import specialists. During the current reporting period, ICE began authorizing CBP user access to use DARTTS to conduct trade transparency analyses. These CBP employees use DARTTS in support of the CBP mission to enforce U.S. trade laws and ensure the collection of all lawfully owed revenue from trade activities. Specifically, CBP uses DARTTS to identify anomalous transactions that may indicate violations of U.S. trade laws. If ICE elects not to open an investigation into these transactions, CBP may initiate administrative enforcement actions to recover delinquent revenue or penalties. Before initiating formal administrative action, CBP will first follow up on the anomalous transactions to determine if they are in fact suspicious and warrant further inquiry. CBP personnel will gather additional facts, verify the accuracy of the DARTTS data, and use their judgment and experience in making that determination. Not all suspicious or anomalous transactions identified in DARTTS will lead to CBP administrative actions.

ICE has now launched a separate web-based instance of the DARTTS system, called "DARTTS World" or "Foreign DARTTS," that is specifically dedicated to use by foreign government partners that operate trade transparency units and have signed a Customs Mutual Assistance Agreement (CMAA) or similar information sharing agreement with the United States. DARTTS World replaces a previous method by which these partners used DARTTS, which involved stand-alone computers located in the foreign partner's office that were loaded with anonymized U.S. trade data as well as the foreign partner's own trade data. ICE has supported the operation of these stand-alone DARTTS terminals by traveling to the foreign partner's office to update software and load new data into the system. To reduce costs and improve security, DARTTS World was created to provide an Internet-based version of DARTTS hosted on the ICE network. In DARTTS World, each foreign partner accesses only the data it is authorized to see as a result of user roles established in the system and managed by ICE. With DARTTS World, there is no change in the data these foreign users can access or in the analytical tools available for their use. Additional information about DARTTS is included in an annex to this report that contains LES information and is being provided separately to Congress.

---

[66] The 2012 DARTTS PIA Update is available at http://www.dhs.gov/privacy-documents-ice.

2. Program Description

ICE maintains DARTTS, which generates leads for and otherwise supports investigations of trade-based money laundering, contraband smuggling, trade fraud, and other import-export crimes led by ICE's Office of Homeland Security Investigations (HSI).[67] DARTTS analyzes trade and financial data to identify statistically anomalous transactions that may warrant investigation. These anomalies are then independently confirmed and further investigated by experienced HSI Special Agents and analysts.

DARTTS is owned and operated by the ICE HSI Trade Transparency Unit (TTU). Trade transparency is the concept of examining U.S. and foreign trade data to identify anomalies in patterns of trade. Such anomalies can indicate trade-based money laundering or other import-export crimes that HSI is responsible for investigating, such as contraband smuggling, trafficking of counterfeit goods, misclassification of goods, and the over- or under-valuation of goods to hide the proceeds of illegal activities. As part of the investigative process, HSI Special Agents and analysts must understand the relationships among importers, exporters, and the financing for a set of trade transactions, to determine which transactions are suspicious and warrant investigation. DARTTS is designed specifically to make this investigative process more efficient by automating the analysis and identification of anomalies.

DARTTS allows HSI to perform research and analysis that is not available in any other ICE system because of the data it contains and the level of detail at which the data can be analyzed.[68] DARTTS does not seek to predict future behavior or "profile" individuals or entities (i.e., identify individuals or entities that meet a certain pattern of behavior pre-determined to be suspect). Instead, it identifies trade and financial transactions that are statistically anomalous based on user-specified queries. HSI Special Agents and analysts follow up on the anomalous transactions to determine if they are in fact suspicious and warrant further investigation. HSI Special Agents and analysts gather additional facts, verify the accuracy of the DARTTS data, and use their judgment and experience in making that determination. Not all anomalies lead to formal investigations.

DARTTS is currently used by HSI Special Agents and analysts who work on TTU investigations at ICE Headquarters or in the ICE HSI field and foreign attaché offices, as well as properly cleared support personnel. DARTTS is accessible to HSI users via the ICE enterprise network. With the 2012 DARTTS update, use of the system was expanded to select CBP Officers and import specialists who conduct trade transparency analyses in furtherance of CBP's mission.

DARTTS World allows foreign partners that have established TTUs in their own governments to access a web-based instance of the DARTTS system hosted on the ICE network. DARTTS World contains only trade data provided by the foreign partners that use the system, and anonymized U.S. trade data that contains trade transactions between the United States and those foreign partners. Foreign trade data is loaded into DARTTS World after the foreign partner uploads the raw data to a secure file transfer protocol (FTP) server at ICE. ICE formats the data and loads it into DARTTS World and tags it so the system will be able to apply the appropriate user access rules to the data.

---

[67] Formerly known as the Office of Investigations, HSI was established during ICE's internal re-organization in June 2010.

[68] For instance, DARTTS allows HSI Special Agents and analysts to view totals for merchandise imports and then sort on any number of variables, such as country of origin, importer name, manufacturer name, or total value.

3. Technology and Methodology

DARTTS uses trade data collected by CBP, other federal agencies and foreign governments, and financial data collected by CBP and the Financial Crimes Enforcement Network (FinCEN). DARTTS data are primarily related to international commercial trade and financial transactions. ICE does not collect information directly from individuals or entities for inclusion in DARTTS. Instead, ICE receives data from the sources listed below via CD-ROM, external storage devices, or electronic data transfers, and loads the data into DARTTS. DARTTS uses COTS software to analyze raw trade and financial data to identify anomalies and other suspicious transactions. The software application is designed for HSI Special Agents and analysts. It enables the analysis of structured and unstructured data using three tools: the drill-down technique,[69] link analysis, and charting and graphing tools that use proprietary statistical algorithms.[70] It also allows non-technical users with investigative experience to analyze large quantities of data and rapidly identify problem areas. The program makes it easier to apply their specific knowledge and expertise to complex sets of data.

DARTTS performs three main types of analysis. It conducts international trade discrepancy analysis by comparing U.S. and foreign import and export data to identify anomalies and discrepancies that warrant further investigation for potential fraud or other illegal activity. It performs unit price analysis by analyzing trade pricing data to identify over- or under-pricing of goods, which may be an indicator of trade-based money laundering. DARTTS also performs financial data analysis by analyzing financial reporting data (the import and export of currency, deposits of currency in financial institutions, reports of suspicious financial activities, and the identities of parties to these transactions) to identify patterns of activity that may indicate money laundering schemes.

DARTTS routinely receives bulk financial and trade information collected by other agencies and foreign governments,[71] hereafter referred to as "raw data." The sources of the raw data are described below. The agencies that provide DARTTS with trade data collect any PII directly from individuals or enterprises completing import-export electronic or paper forms.[72] Agencies that provide DARTTS with financial data receive PII from individuals and institutions, such as banks, that are required to complete certain financial reporting forms.[73] PII in the raw data is necessary to link related transactions together. It is also necessary to identify persons or entities that should be investigated further.

---

[69] The drill-down system allows HSI Special Agents and analysts to quickly find, analyze, share, and document suspicious patterns in large amounts of data, and to continually observe and analyze patterns in data at any point. HSI Special Agents and analysts can also connect from one dataset within DARTTS to another, to see whether the suspicious individuals, entities, or patterns occur elsewhere.

[70] DARTTS provides HSI Special Agents and analysts the means to represent data graphically in graphs, charts, or tables to aid in the visual identification of anomalous transactions. DARTTS does not create new records to be stored in DARTTS.

[71] Foreign trade data may include: names of importers, exporters, and brokers; addresses of importers and exporters; Importer IDs; Exporter IDs; Broker IDs; and Manufacturer IDs.

[72] U.S. trade data includes the following PII: names and addresses (home or business) of importers, exporters, brokers, and consignees; Importer and Exporter IDs (e.g., an individual's or entity's Social Security or Tax Identification Number); Broker IDs; and Manufacturer IDs.

[73] U.S. financial data includes the following PII: names of individuals engaging in financial transactions that are reportable under the Bank Secrecy Act (BSA), 31 U.S.C. §§ 5311-5332, (e.g., cash transactions over $10,000); addresses; Social Security/Taxpayer Identification Numbers; passport number and country of issuance; bank account numbers; party names and addresses; and owner names and addresses.

HSI Special Agents with experience conducting financial, money laundering, and trade fraud investigations use completed analyses to identify possible criminal activity and provide support to field investigators. HSI Special Agents and analysts at ICE Headquarters assigned to the TTU refer the results of DARTTS analyses to ICE HSI field offices as part of an investigative referral package to initiate or support a criminal investigation. HSI Special Agents and analysts in domestic field offices can also independently generate leads and subsequent investigations using DARTTS analyses. HSI Special Agents in attaché offices at U.S. embassies and consulates abroad have access to DARTTS on stand-alone terminals. These HSI Special Agents use DARTTS to conduct analyses in support of financial, money laundering, and trade fraud investigations, and to respond to inquiries from partner-country TTUs with whom ICE shares anonymized U.S. trade data.

4. Data Sources

All raw data in DARTTS is provided by other U.S. agencies and foreign governments, and is divided into the following broad categories: U.S. trade data, foreign trade data, U.S. financial data, and law enforcement records. U.S. trade data in DARTTS is (1) import data in the form of an extract from ACS, which CBP collects from individuals and entities importing merchandise into the United States who complete CBP Form 7501 (Entry Summary) or provide electronic manifest information via ACS; (2) EEI; and (3) publicly available aggregated U.S. export data (i.e., data that does not include PII) purchased by ICE from the U.S. Department of Commerce.[74] In FY13, ICE plans to incorporate a data module with bill of lading data into the DARTTS enterprise version. This information includes consignee name and address, shipper name and address, container number, carrier, and bill of lading. It is collected by CBP via the AMS, and is provided to ICE through CD-ROM, external storage devices, or electronic data transfers for uploading into DARTTS. The bill of lading module is included in the 2010 DARTTS PIA update.[75]

Foreign import and export data in DARTTS is provided to ICE by partner countries pursuant to a CMAA or other similar agreement. Certain countries provide trade data that has been stripped of PII. Other countries provide complete trade data, which includes any individuals' names and other identifying information that may be contained in the trade records.

ICE receives U.S. financial data from FinCEN for uploading into DARTTS. This data is in the form of the following financial transaction reports: CMIRs; Currency Transaction Reports (deposits or withdrawals of more than $10,000 in currency into or from depository institutions and casinos and card clubs); Suspicious Activity Reports (information regarding suspicious financial transactions within depository institutions, money services businesses,[76] the securities and futures industry, and casinos and card clubs); Reports of Cash Payments over $10,000 Received in a Trade or Business (reports of merchandise purchased with $10,000 or more in

---

[74] This dataset is known as the U.S. Exports of Merchandise Dataset and is further described (including a complete list of data fields) on the U.S. Department of Commerce website available at http://www.census.gov/foreign-trade/reference/products/catalog/expDVD html.

[75] The 2010 DARTTS PIA Update is available at http://www.dhs.gov/privacy-documents-ice.

[76] Money services businesses are required by the BSA to complete and submit Suspicious Activity Reports to FinCEN. 31 U.S.C. § 5318. They include money transmitters; issuers; redeemers and sellers of money orders and travelers' checks; and check cashers and currency exchangers. FinCEN administers the BSA, which requires depository institutions and other industries vulnerable to money laundering to take precautions against financial crime, including reporting financial transactions possibly indicative of money laundering. 31 U.S.C. §§ 5311-5330.

currency); and data provided in Reports of Foreign Bank and Financial Accounts (FBAR) (reports by U.S. persons who have financial interest in, or signature or other authority over, foreign financial accounts in excess of $10,000).

ICE receives law enforcement records from two sources. First, ICE loads into DARTTS the publicly available SDN List, which is a list of individuals and companies owned or controlled by, or acting on behalf of, targeted countries. The list also contains information about foreign individuals, groups and entities, such as terrorists and narcotics traffickers designated under programs that are not country-specific. Their assets are blocked and U.S. persons and entities are generally prohibited from dealing with them. This dataset is compiled and maintained by the U.S. Treasury Department's Office of Foreign Assets Control (OFAC) and is also publicly available on the OFAC website.[77] The inclusion of the SDN List into DARTTS allows HSI users to rapidly determine, while using DARTTS to conduct analysis, if international trade and/or financial transactions with a specially designated individual or entity are being conducted, thus providing HSI with the ability to take appropriate actions in a timely and more efficient manner.

The second source that ICE loads into DARTTS are subject records created by HSI users from CBP's TECS database. HSI subject records pertain to persons, vehicles, vessels, businesses, aircraft, and 'things' (houses, etc.). Having HSI subject records in DARTTS allows HSI Special Agents and analysts to quickly determine if an entity that is being researched in DARTTS is already part of a pending investigation or was involved in an investigation that is now closed.

DARTTS itself is the source of analyses of the raw data produced using COTS software analytical tools within the system. DARTTS also creates extracts of U.S. trade data that has been stripped of PII, and provides those extracts to partner countries that operate their own TTUs and have DARTTS terminals set up within their customs agencies' offices. This trade data is shared only with partner countries that have entered into a CMAA or other similar agreement with the United States. U.S. financial data in DARTTS is not shared with partner countries.

5. Efficacy

DARTTS has proven to be an effective tool for HSI in identifying criminal activity. Through the utilization of DARTTS, domestic field offices and foreign attaché offices have the ability to initiate and enhance criminal cases related to trade-based money laundering and other financial crimes. Information derived from DARTTS has been essential in several criminal prosecutions and enforcement actions both domestically and abroad. For example, using information gathered through financial queries in DARTTS, HSI TTU revealed that bulk currency was moving into Miami from Colombia and transiting the United States from Miami to the United Kingdom and, ultimately, to Germany. The bulk currency was suspected to be proceeds of the European drug market. As a result of this TTU-generated lead, currency valued at 12 million U.S. dollars (USD) was seized by HSI and CBP. Further analysis using DARTTS led to an additional seizure valued at nine million USD by HSI and the U.S. Drug Enforcement Administration at Miami International Airport.

DARTTS has also been used in support of enforcement actions. For example, HSI Miami and HSI Attaché Buenos Aires initiated an operation aimed at targeting transnational crime organizations involved in money laundering, trafficking of counterfeit merchandise, intellectual

---

[77] *See* www.treasury.gov/ofac.

property rights violations, and contraband smuggling schemes from Paraguay, Brazil, and Argentina to the United States. Working in conjunction with its foreign counterparts, HSI TTU used DARTTS to identify trade anomalies for numerous companies and suspect entities targeted by this operation. The operation culminated in the convictions of three violators and their companies, as well as 250 cargo seizures worth approximately 120 million USD.

6. Laws and Regulations

ICE is authorized to conduct these law enforcement activities under 18 U.S.C. § 545 (Smuggling goods into the United States); 18 U.S.C. § 554 (Smuggling goods from the United States); 18 U.S.C. § 371 (Conspiracy); 18 U.S.C. § 1956 (Laundering of Monetary Instruments); 19 U.S.C. § 1484 (Entry of Merchandise); 50 U.S.C. § 1701 et seq. (the International Emergency Economic Powers Act); and its broad law enforcement authorities under 19 U.S.C. § 1589a. DHS is authorized to maintain documentation of these activities pursuant to 19 U.S.C. § 2071 note (Cargo Information) and 44 U.S.C. § 3101 (Records Management by Agency Heads; General Duties). Information in DARTTS is regulated under the Privacy Act of 1974,[78] the Trade Secrets Act,[79] and the Bank Secrecy Act (BSA).

7. Privacy Impact and Privacy Protections

ICE does not use DARTTS to make unevaluated automated decisions about individuals, and DARTTS data is never used directly as evidence to prosecute crimes. DARTTS is solely an analytical tool used to identify anomalies. It is incumbent upon the HSI Special Agent or analyst to further investigate the reason for an anomaly. HSI Special Agents and analysts gather additional facts, verify the accuracy of the DARTTS data, and use their judgment and experience to determine whether an anomaly is in fact suspicious and warrants further investigation for criminal violations. HSI Special Agents and analysts are required to obtain and verify the original source data from the agency that collected the information to prevent inaccurate information from propagating. All information obtained from DARTTS is independently verified before it is acted upon or included in an HSI investigative or analytical report.

DARTTS data is generally subject to access and amendment requests under the Privacy Act and FOIA, unless a statutory exemption covering specific data applies. U.S. and foreign government agencies that collect information uploaded into DARTTS are responsible for providing appropriate notice on the forms used to collect the information, or through other forms of public notice, such as SORNs.[80] DARTTS will coordinate requests for access or to amend data with the original data owner. ICE published a PIA Update and SORN for DARTTS on April 2, 2012, and September 4, 2012, respectively.[81]

The information in DARTTS is obtained from other governmental organizations that collect the data under specific legislative authorities. DARTTS cannot independently verify the accuracy of

---

[78] 5 U.S.C. § 552a

[79] 18 U.S.C. § 1905.

[80] The following SORNs are published in the Federal Register and describe the raw data ICE receives from U.S. agencies for use in DARTTS: for FinCEN Information, Suspicious Activity Report System (Treasury/FinCEN .002) and BSA Reports System (Treasury/FinCEN .003); for Commerce Department Information, Individuals Identified in Export Transactions System (Commerce/ITA-1); and for CBP Information, Automated Commercial Environment/International Trade Data System (ACE/ITDS) (DHS/CBP-001).

[81] DARTTS is covered by the SORN for the ICE Trade Transparency and Analysis Research (TTAR) system of records. The SORN is available on the Privacy Office website at http://www.dhs.gov/privacy and in the Federal Register at 77 FR 171 (Sep. 4, 2012).

all of the data that it receives. The owner of the source data is responsible for maintaining and checking the accuracy of its own data. In many instances, the data ultimately loaded into DARTTS is highly accurate because it is collected directly from the individual. In other instances, however, the data about individuals is provided to a governmental organization by a third party. In the event that errors are found, the DARTTS system owner must notify the agency that originally collected the data. FinCEN currently provides ICE with corrections to existing data, which are then uploaded into DARTTS. ICE does not, however, receive data corrections on trade data.

DARTTS re-certified its C&A and was granted a three-year authority to operate from DHS IT Security on April 22, 2010. In 2010, DARTTS completed its transition to the ICE enterprise network and is now maintained within the secure DHS network firewall. Any violations of system security or suspected criminal activity will be reported to the DHS Office of Inspector General, to the Office of the Information System Security Manager team in accordance with the DHS security standards, and to the ICE Office of Professional Responsibility.

All DARTTS users are assigned unique user IDs and passwords. Audit trails are used to track the date and time of login and sequences of users' actions and queries. New audit trail functionality has been implemented to provide an even more detailed trail and a higher level of integrity and accountability. The new audit trail features for the DARTTS enterprise version automatically track each action that occurs in the system, the date and time the action occurs, and which user performed the action. Only authorized personnel have access to audit trails, which are kept for a minimum of 90 days. Audit trails are reviewed by DARTTS system administrators and the Information System Security Officer. The system administrator also maintains a spreadsheet record of the receipt or distribution of sensitive information on electronic media.[82]

Access to DARTTS is granted on a case-by-case basis by the TTU Network Administrator. Access is limited to HSI users working on TTU investigations and properly cleared support personnel, select CBP Officers and import specialists, and foreign government customs officers and import specialists when ICE has diplomatic agreements or arrangements with that government's TTU. All individuals who are granted system use privileges are properly cleared to access information within DARTTS and take system-specific training, as well as annual privacy and security training, that stresses the importance of authorized use of personal data in government systems.

In 2009, NARA approved a record retention period for the information maintained in DARTTS. ICE maintains records in DARTTS for five years and then archives them for five additional years, for a total retention period of 10 years. As noted in the 2012 DARTTS PIA Update,[83] ICE intends to request NARA approval to modify that retention period to retain the data for a total of ten years in the system. A retention policy change from five to 10 years' worth of data in the system would provide more useful analytical results to DARTTS users and would permit them to view transactions of ongoing trade-based or financial fraud over a more significant period of time. The proposed 10-year retention period for records is necessary to create a data set large enough to effectively identify anomalies and patterns of behavior in trade transactions. Original

---

[82] DARTTS receives CD-ROMs and other external storage media provided by other agencies. Once data from CD-ROMs or other external storage media is loaded onto DARTTS, the TTU Network Administrator stores them in the secured server room located in the TTU offices at ICE Headquarters until the retention period has elapsed, at which point they are destroyed.
[83] Available at http://www.dhs.gov/privacy-documents-ice.

compact discs containing raw data will be retained for five years to ensure data integrity and for system maintenance.

IV. CONCLUSION

The DHS Privacy Office is pleased to provide the Congress its seventh comprehensive report on DHS data mining activities. The Congress has authorized the Department to engage in data mining in furtherance of the DHS mission while protecting privacy. The Office has reviewed the programs described in this report, using the compliance documentation process it requires for all DHS programs and systems to ensure that necessary privacy protections have been implemented. The DHS Privacy Office remains vigilant in its oversight of all Department programs and systems, including those that involve data mining.

V. APPENDIX

A.

Acronym List	
ABI	Automated Broker Interface
ACAS	Air Cargo Advance Screening
ACE	Automated Commercial Environment
ACE/ITDS	Automated Commercial Environment/International Trade Data System
ACS	Automated Commercial System
ADIS	Arrival and Departure Information System
AES	Automated Export System
AFI	Analytical Framework for Intelligence
AMS	Automated Manifest System
APIS	Advance Passenger Information System
ATO	Authorization to Operate
ATS	Automated Targeting System
ATSA	Aviation and Transportation Security Act
ATS-AT	Automated Targeting System—Outbound Module
ATS-N	Automated Targeting System—Inbound Module
ATS-L	Automated Targeting System—Land Module
ATS-P	Automated Targeting System—Passenger Module
ATS-TF	Automated Targeting System—Targeting Framework
BCI	Border Crossing Information
BSA	Bank Secrecy Act
C&A	Certification and Accreditation
CAFES	CBP Automated Forms Entry System
CBP	U.S. Customs and Border Protection
CCD	Consolidated Consular Database
CCRA	Canadian Customs and Revenue
CMAA	Customs Mutual Assistance Agreement
CMIR	The Report of International Transportation of Currency or Monetary Instruments Form
COTP	Captains of the Port
COTS	Commercial Off-The-Shelf
DARTTS	Data Analysis and Research for Trade Transparency System
DCID	Director of Central Intelligence Directive
DHS	Department of Homeland Security
DMV	Department of Motor Vehicles
DOJ	Department of Justice
DoS	Department of State
EBSVERA	Enhanced Border Security and Visa Entry Reform Act of 2002
EEI	Electronic Export Information
ESTA	Electronic System for Travel Authorization

	Acronym List
FBAR	Report of Foreign Bank and Financial Accounts
FBI	Federal Bureau of Investigation
FinCEN	Department of the Treasury Financial Crimes Enforcement Network
FIPPs	Fair Information Practice Principles
FISMA	Federal Information Security Management Act
FOIA	Freedom of Information Act
FTP	File Transfer Protocol
FY	Fiscal Year
HSI	ICE Homeland Security Investigations Directorate
HSPD	Homeland Security Presidential Directive
I&A	Office of Intelligence and Analysis
ICE	United States Immigration and Customs Enforcement
IEEPA	International Emergency Economic Powers Act
INA	Immigration and Nationality Act
IOC	Interagency Operations Center
IOFS	Intelligence and Operations Framework System
IRTPA	Intelligence Reform and Terrorism Prevention Act of 2004
IT	Information Technology
LES	Law Enforcement Sensitive
NARA	National Archives and Records Administration
NCIC	National Crime Information Center
NIIS	Nonimmigrant Information System
NTC	National Targeting Center
OFAC	Department of the Treasury Office of Foreign Asset Control
PCR	Privacy Compliance Review
PIA	Privacy Impact Assessment
PII	Personally Identifiable Information
PL2+	Protection Level 2+
PNR	Passenger Name Record
PPOC	Privacy Point of Contact
PTA	Privacy Threshold Analysis
RFI	Request for Information
SAFE Port Act	Security and Accountability for Every Port Act
SAVI	Suspect and Violator Indices
SED	Shippers' Export Declaration
SELC	System Engineering Life Cycle
SEVIS	Student and Exchange Visitor Information System
SDN	Specially Designated Nationals
SORN	System of Records Notice
SSI	Sensitive Security Information
TRACS	Technical Reconciliation Analysis Classification System
TRIP	Traveler Redress Inquiry Program

Acronym List	
TSA	Transportation Security Administration
TSC	FBI Terrorist Screening Center
TSDB	Terrorist Screening Database
TTAR	Transaction and Analysis Research System
TTU	ICE Office of Investigations Trade Transparency Unit
USA PATRIOT Act	Uniting and Strengthening America by Providing Appropriate Tools Required to Intercept and Obstruct Terrorism Act
U.S.	United States
U.S.C.	United States Code
USCIS	United States Citizenship and Immigration Services
USCG	United States Coast Guard
USD	United States Dollar
US-VISIT	United States Visitor and Immigrant Status Indicator Technology
VSPTS-Net	Visa Security Program Tracking System
VWP	Visa Waiver Program